JANE AUSTEN

A Life From Beginning to End

Copyright © 2018 by Hourly History.

All rights reserved.

Table of Contents

Introduction
The Austen Family
A Young Writer Emerges
Forced to Move
Austen's Romances
Sense and Sensibility
Pride and Prejudice
Emma, the Unlikeable Heroine
Jane's Mysterious Illness
Last Days and Death
Conclusion

Introduction

The years between 1714 and 1830 marked England's Georgian era, when George I, George II, George III, and George IV held the country's throne. During this time, the novel was growing as a new literary form. Daniel Defoe wrote *Robinson Crusoe* in 1719, and Sir Walter Scott began writing his historically inspired novels at the beginning of the 1800s. Yet while these novels were full of adventure and sweeping in scope, as the eighteenth century came to end, Jane Austen had started writing novels that instead painted the world "with so fine a brush," focusing on the relationships, families, and social lives of people much like those she knew. She was interested in developing her characters and their interactions with one another, stating that "three or four families in a country village is the very thing to work on."

Despite the seemingly small scale of her work, Austen's observations about human nature have proven so accurate and entertaining that her books continue to be beloved 200 years after they were written. Writer W. Somerset Maugham once said of Austen's work, "Nothing very much happens in her books, and yet, when you come to the bottom of a page, you eagerly turn it to learn what will happen next. Nothing very much does and again you eagerly turn the page." Even the famous author of *Harry Potter*, J.K. Rowling, said in 2003 that Jane Austen is her favorite writer: "I've read all her books so many times I've lost count." Austen's novels have been turned into numerous adaptations for the screen, spreading their enduring popularity beyond those who have read the books.

Though her novels have become well known as classics of literature, Jane Austen's life poses challenges to uncover. At the time of her death, her family remembered her as a dear sister, daughter, and aunt, not as an author. Consequently, many of the letters she wrote throughout her life were lost or destroyed. Despite this, enough records remain to give us a picture of Austen's life, a picture that also helps us understand her development as a writer and that enlivens our readings of her beloved novels.

Chapter One

The Austen Family

"If Cassandra's head had been going to be cut off, then Jane would have hers cut off too."

—Cassandra Austen, Jane's mother

George Austen, a man who came from a line of respected and wealthy wool merchants but who had little money himself, attended St. John's College, Oxford during the mid-1700s. He most likely met Cassandra Leigh, the daughter of the rector of All Souls College, Oxford, while he was there. The two married on April 26, 1764. The same day they were married, they left for Steventon, Hampshire, in southern England, where George had received the living for the Steventon parish due to a family connection. The house was run down and unlivable, so the couple lived in nearby Deane for several years. There, Cassandra gave birth to the first three of their children: James, George, and Edward. James would become known for his writing talents. George suffered from epilepsy, may have had learning disabilities, and was deaf. He was sent to live and be cared for by a nearby family; it is uncertain if this was the typical pattern of care for children such as George who were born into a family of the gentry.

The family was able to move into Steventon in 1768. Steventon was known for its hedgerows, which lined gardens and meadows as well as the edges of properties. The hedgerows—trees and bushes—made Steventon a peaceful place, with benches for ladies to rest on and plenty of wildflowers. Here, the Austen family continued to grow. The fourth son Henry was born in 1771, followed by Cassandra, Francis, and then Jane on December 16, 1775. On the birth of his second daughter, George Austen remarked that she would make a good "future companion" for her older sister Cassie.

Reverend Austen not only wrote sermons and cared for his congregation but also ran a boys' boarding school, where he taught his students Latin and Greek. He was also in charge of the family's Cheesedown Farm. Both of these endeavors helped to add to his income as a clergyman—which would have been no more than a few hundred pounds a year—and support his family. George Austen always made time to read to his children from his large collection of books; he also owned a microscope and was interested in science, as was common among clergymen of the time.

Jane's mother worked hard as well—she not only mothered seven children but also ran the household, washing the linens, cooking, sewing clothes, and performing outside duties like taking care of the cow and chickens. Beyond this, she was expected to help bring food, blankets, and other necessities to the poor in the community, a task which Jane would have joined in when she was old enough. Along with her hard work, Cassandra

Austen was known for composing clever poems and playing the piano.

When Jane was just three, in the spring of 1779, George Austen's cousin and his wife, Thomas and Catherine Knight, came to visit. They invited Jane's older brother Edward to join them as they traveled during the summer. In the same year, the youngest Austen, Charles, was born. Soon after, James, who was 14, followed in his father's footsteps by leaving for St. John's College in Oxford, having received a scholarship due to connections of his mother's. This was not an unusual age to start college, as boys began whenever they were academically ready—some were younger than James.

Just a few years later, the Knights made the Austens an offer: the wealthy couple wanted Edward to become their heir since they had no children of their own. George and Cassandra Austen agreed, seeing an excellent opportunity for Edward. When Edward was 16, the adoption took place, and he moved to Kent to live on the Knights' large estate. He always remained on good terms with the Austen family.

In 1783, ten-year-old Cassandra was ready to go off to school. Jane, three years younger, went too—not because she was old enough, but because she insisted on doing everything Cassie did. George Austen's prediction that his daughters would become good friends had proven to be true. The two girls, along with one of their cousins, Jane Cooper, went to a school in Oxford run by a Mrs. Cawley. While boys went to school to learn subjects like math, science, and classical languages, girls mainly practiced penmanship and needlework and learned to act in the ways that society expected from a lady. There were no regulations for schools of this kind, and any woman who needed to earn extra money might open one in her home. Consequently, in some of them, girls (and boys in similar boys' schools) lived in unhealthy conditions, with crowded quarters and inadequate food. The children's parents often did not know what was going on.

Mrs. Cawley, who ran the school where the Austen sisters went, took her students to Southampton in the summer of 1783 just as a disease that may have been typhus or diphtheria broke out in the area. Soon the sisters and their cousin were all sick, and Mrs. Cawley refused to let her students send letters to their families to alert them to the situation. At last, when Jane Austen's condition continued to worsen, Jane Cooper decided to sneak a letter out to her mother. Mrs. Austen and Mrs. Cooper soon arrived to care for their daughters. Jane nearly died but eventually made a full recovery. Mrs. Cooper, however, caught the disease and soon died.

Jane Cooper became a more constant part of the Austen sisters' life after her mother's death, often staying at Steventon. For one year, from 1785 to 1786, the girls went to a school where conditions were better, even if they did not learn much because the teacher preferred talking about actors rather than doing lessons. Back home at age 11, Jane took music lessons, developing her lifelong love of playing the piano. She also read, enjoying books like Samuel Richardson's *Sir Charles Grandison* and Fanny Burney's *Cecilia*.

In 1786, another relative entered Jane's life. Her cousin Eliza had grown up in India and then married a French count. Eliza's husband had then sent her to England to have their first child. Count Jean-Francois Capot de Feuillide was busy working on the massive undertaking of draining swamplands that made of part of his estate, and he stayed in France while his wife went to England. To Jane, meeting the fashionable and accomplished Eliza was like meeting a character from a book. Eliza also felt affection for her young cousin; she encouraged Jane at the piano and gave her French children's book so that Jane could practice French.

At around this time, Jane began to write stories. Becoming an author, for a woman of Jane's time, was not considered a proper and ladylike endeavor. Some women—such as Ann Radcliffe, who pioneered the gothic novel, or the daring Mary Wollstonecraft, who wrote *A Vindication of the Rights of Women*—published under their own names. Others published their work anonymously or under pen names to avoid attention and accusations of "taking on airs."

Jane's writing was at this stage done mainly for the amusement of her family. She experimented with drama and novels, and she even wrote a humorous history of England which she described as being written "by a partial, prejudiced, and ignorant Historian," and which her sister illustrated. At 14, she dedicated the novella *Love and Freindship* (Jane's spelling) to her cousin Eliza. She collected her favorite writings into three notebooks. These works, spanning from when Jane was 11 to 18, are called

Juvenilia. They reveal that she was already beginning to develop the keen observations of her society and sense of irony that would characterize her mature novels.

Chapter Two

A Young Writer Emerges

"And it is therefore most probable that our indifference will soon be mutual, unless his regard, which appeared to spring from knowing nothing of me at first, is best supported by never seeing me."

—Jane Austen on Reverend Samuel Blackall

In 1788, when Jane was 12 years old, her family traveled to Kent to visit relatives. Among the relatives she met on this trip was a woman named Philadelphia Walter. Philadelphia recorded her impressions of the two young Austen sisters: she thought Cassandra was pretty, but Jane was not. Additionally, she faulted Jane for appearing "whimsical and affected," making clever remarks throughout the dinner.

At the risk of judgment from people like Philadelphia, Jane continued to exercise her cleverness in her writing. She dedicated another novella, *Jack and Alice*, to her younger brother Francis, whom the family called Frank. Around this time, when Frank was 14, he graduated from the Royal Naval Academy and sailed for the East Indies—it would be five years before he returned to England. The baby of the family, Charles, soon followed Frank's path into the Naval Academy. Jane's brother Edward married, his wife a baronet's daughter named Elizabeth Bridges. Jane's oldest brother James, finishing his education at St. John's College, became a clergyman. He married a general's daughter, Anne Mathew, in 1792, and the two moved to Deane. Cassie would soon also be engaged—her fiancé, Tom Fowle, was a poor clergyman, and since Cassandra could only bring little money to the marriage, they would have to wait years before marrying.

Jane, in 1792, was 16 years old. By this time even Philadelphia Walters admitted her to be "greatly improved . . . in manners as in person." She was known for her liveliness—one neighbor remembered her face as having "sparkling eyes not large but joyous and intelligent." She was tall and thin according to various witnesses who remembered her, and her brother Henry said she was a very good dancer.

Jane and her family spent time with other families of their social standing, such as lawyers or doctors. Among these friends were the Bigg family, the children of a landowning widower who did not need to work. Cassie and Jane were friends with Catherine, Elizabeth, and Alethea Bigg. Two other friends, Martha and Mary Lloyd, were the daughters of a clergyman's widow. Mary had lived through smallpox and had the scars from the disease marking her face. She was Jane's age, but Jane liked the older Martha better, as she had a better sense of humor. Mary and Martha had another sister who had married one of the Fowles. The Austens were also friends with other clergymen's families, such as the Lefroys, who lived in the nearby village of Ashe. Reverend George Lefroy's wife

Anne wrote poetry, read avidly, and even memorized passages of Shakespeare. She offered Jane her encouragement as a fellow writer.

The Austen family continued to grow with the birth of a daughter, Anna, to James and Anne in 1793. The same year, Edward and Elizabeth had a daughter named Fanny. Henry Austen, four years older than Jane, had started at Oxford by this point, intending to follow in the footsteps of his father and oldest brother and become a clergyman. But when war between England and France broke out in 1793, impulsive Henry dropped his studies to join the Oxford militia. Within the next year, he had traveled to Portsmouth to guard French prisoners.

Jane, as she watched her siblings' lives move forward, must have dreamed about moving on to the next step of her own life. In the registry of her father's church, she recorded her daydreams: "Henry Frederic Howard Fitzwilliam of London and Jane Austen of Steventon" and "Edmund Arthur William Mortimer of Liverpool and Jane Austen of Steventon." She even wrote, "Jack Smith and Jane Smith late Austen, in the presence Jack Smith, Jane Smith." Reverend George Austen left Jane's entries unchanged amidst the serious records of the marriages, births, and deaths of his parishioners.

Soon some excitement came to Jane's life in the form of a young man named Tom Lefroy. He came to Steventon in December 1795 to visit his aunt and uncle, Anne and George Lefroy, for Christmas. Jane had met him previously at a ball hosted by the Biggs. Tom and Jane were soon giving each other more attention than was proper in their strictly ordered society. In a letter to Cassie (the earliest of Jane's surviving letters), who was in Berkshire with the Fowles, Jane described her and Tom's conduct as "everything most profligate and shocking in the way of dancing and sitting down together."

Another ball was soon to take place, held by the Lefroys themselves, and Jane happily expected that Tom would ask her to marry him on that occasion. But the Lefroys intervened, whisking him back to London before the ball; they wanted him to marry a woman who could provide wealth to help Tom's prospects for moving up in the world, and Jane had no money. The romance was over—that was the last Jane ever saw of Tom Lefroy. Tom went on to marry an Irish heiress, serve in Parliament, and become lord chief justice of Ireland.

During her brief romance, and even before she met Tom, Jane had been working on a novel called *Elinor and Marianne*, told through letters. In the story, one sister, Marianne—much like Jane had done with Tom—relies on her heart to lead her and ignores the more prudent Elinor's counsel for caution and propriety.

Less than two years later, perhaps as a kind of apology, Anne Lefroy introduced Jane to another potential suitor, the young Reverend Samuel Blackall. While Blackall was apparently interested, Jane was not. Later, when he married someone else, Jane commented on how he seemed to perceive himself as perfect and how he would need a wife who was "of a silent turn and rather ignorant, but naturally intelligent and wishing to learn."

At the same time, Jane was hard at work on a new novel entitled *First Impressions*. As with *Elinor and Marianne*, Jane's second novel as an adult began to show more serious and thoughtful character development and a more realistic plot than she had written in her *Juvenilia*. Her family loved *First Impressions*, as did her friends. Jane's father even sent it off anonymously to a publisher in London, Thomas Cadell, thinking it ought to be published. Cadell turned it down, but Jane kept on writing.

Chapter Three

Forced to Move

"The first view of Bath in fine weather does not answer my expectations ... the appearance of the place ... was all vapour, shadow, smoke, and confusion."

—Jane Austen

During the years that Jane was disappointed by Tom Lefroy and disappointed Samuel Blackall in turn, several misfortunes struck members of her family. In 1795, James' wife Anne suddenly died; their daughter, Anna, moved to the Austens' house in Steventon. The same year, Cassie's fiancé, Tom Fowle, joined the army and was sent to be a chaplain in the West Indies; when he returned, he hoped to at last be well situated to marry Cassandra, but the separation would be over a year and the location dangerous. During the next year, Jane's now happily married cousin Jane Cooper was in a carriage accident on the Isle of Wight and died. In 1797, Cassandra expected her fiancé to return home but instead received the news that he had died of yellow fever.

The year of 1797 marked the weddings of two of Jane's brothers, both of which could take place only because of family tragedies. Henry Austen married his cousin, Eliza de Feuillide (marriage between first cousins was not seen as a problem in Jane's time). Eliza had gone through many difficulties, from the slow death of her mother by cancer to the death of her husband, the count, in the French Revolution. He had escaped when peasants destroyed his estate but was caught and put to death by the guillotine in Paris when he tried to save an elderly woman from jail through bribery.

Henry first asked Eliza to marry him in 1795, a year after the count's death. She said no, and also refused the widowed James, who asked her later. At last, she agreed to marry Henry, and the wedding took place in 1797. Henry, now an army captain, loved not only Eliza but also her son Hastings. This touched Eliza, who was doing her best to care for Hastings herself even though he experienced severe developmental delays.

James eventually remarried in 1797, taking Mary Lloyd as his wife. Jane never liked the humorless Mary, and little Anna, who now returned to live with her father and stepmother, missed her aunts and the home at Steventon. She still saw them often, though, as Jane and Cassie enjoyed walking together from Steventon to Deane to visit Anna and her parents.

Edward and Elizabeth were doing quite well by this time and already had five children. In 1799, they invited Jane and her mother to go to Bath with them. This was an exciting opportunity for Jane—Bath was not only a popular, bustling resort town and a destination for health cures but also a place where young men and women could meet a wide variety of potential matches. There were frequent concerts, plays, and dances. However, Jane found she did not like Bath as much as she might have expected. The outdoor concerts were not of high quality, which was disappointing to the accomplished pianist. After leaving Bath, Jane and her mother traveled through Gloucestershire and Surrey to visit some friends and relatives.

Back in Steventon, Jane resumed the usual pace of life she had always known, settling back into writing. She revised *Elinor and Marianne*, and at this time moved away from the format of letters that she had previously used and told the story in a narrative style. She changed the name, too, now calling the novel *Sense and Sensibility*. Additionally, Bath had given her the idea for a novel set there, and she had made careful observations during her time in the town. She began work on a story she called *Susan*, about a girl who is an avid reader of gothic novels and imagines similar dramatic events unfolding all around her.

A surviving letter to Cassandra—who was off helping Edward and Elizabeth as Elizabeth gave birth to the couple's sixth child—reports that Jane also went to a ball in the fall of 1800; she had plenty of observant and witty comments to make about the other attendees. During Cassandra's absence, Jane went to visit her good friend Martha Lloyd, who had moved and now lived 20 miles away—a much more significant distance in 1800 than now. She and Martha returned to Steventon together. There, Jane received a shock: her parents announced that Reverend Austen would retire, James and Mary would move into the Steventon parsonage, and the rest of the family would move to Bath. As a single woman, Jane had no choice but to move with her parents. She was so surprised and deeply upset by the news—which meant she would move far from the only place she had lived and the people she knew—that uncharacteristically, she fainted.

Chapter Four

Austen's Romances

"Single women have a dreadful propensity for being poor, which is one very strong argument in favour of matrimony."

—Jane Austen

There is no record of Jane's thoughts on the move from when she first heard the plan in November of 1800 to the following January. Then, in a letter to Cassandra, Jane reveals that she has become accustomed to the idea of moving and begins to look for the positives. Yet she is sad about seeing the Austen possessions sold, especially about seeing items go to James and Mary even before the family had left. She was especially annoyed at a hint that she ought to give her own cabinet to her niece Anna, writing to Cassandra, "I do not choose to have generosity dictated to me."

Though Jane did not love Bath, the town offered a location from which the Austens could more easily travel to other resort towns in the summers. They ventured to Dawlish and Teignmouth, and on the coast of Wales, Jane used a bathing machine as was customary for her day to enter the sea so that she could try wading. More than once, the Austens visited Lyme, a seaside town surrounded by tall, white cliffs. There, Jane enjoyed balls and walks along the harbor wall known as the Cobb.

It was on the Devonshire coast in 1801 or 1802 that one of the lingering mysteries of Jane Austen's life took place. There, Jane became acquainted with a man who must have been charming and intelligent based on later remarks of Cassandra's, which are the only evidence that remains of this episode of Jane's life. The two formed an attachment, and when he or the Austens were about to depart, he asked where the Austens would vacation the next summer, presumably with the intention of meeting them again. Cassandra expected the man to propose to Jane and thought Jane would accept. But before they could see him again, the family heard that the gentleman had died. The identity of Jane's seaside suitor remains a mystery. Though one author suggested it might have been Reverend Samuel Blackall, this does not necessarily seem to fit with Blackall's life, as he lived until 1842. None of Jane's letters from this time survive to hint at the man's possible identity.

Jane and Cassie also made long trips to visit relatives and friends without their parents. They frequently spent time with Edward and Elizabeth at their home, Godmersham Park. Edward had by this time changed his last name to Knight, as the terms of his adoption and inheritance dictated. Henry, who was now a banker, and Eliza also regularly visited Godmersham Park. Eliza's son Hastings, however, had died at the age of 15.

While Jane enjoyed the luxuries of life at Edward's house, with its grand library and lovely walking paths and gardens, she did not visit as often as Cassandra. Elizabeth seemed to like Cassandra better, and it is possible that she felt some jealousy of Jane, who was recognized by the family for her many talents. Edward and Elizabeth's daughter Fanny further suggested that Jane "was not so refined as she ought to have been from her talent." Jane, for her part, was unimpressed by the Knights' wealthy friends, whom she found uninteresting. Instead, she befriended Anne Sharp, the Knights' intelligent governess, who would remain a lifelong friend.

Jane and Cassandra made another visit in 1802, this time to see their friends Alethea, Catherine, and Elizabeth Bigg. The Bigg sisters' younger brother, 21-year-old Harris Bigg-Wither, was the heir to his father's large estate and was therefore unconcerned about marrying for money. In December 1802, he asked Jane to marry him, and she said yes. For 27-year-old Jane, nearing the end of her marriageable years and with no money of her own, it was a match that promised a secure future not only for herself but also for Cassandra. Everyone was pleased by Jane's choice, and the party spent the evening celebrating.

By the following morning, however, Jane had rethought her decision. She did not love Harris even though they were friends, and he was not in love with her either; marriage between them would be more like a social contract. Jane felt she could not live with this. She asked to speak to Harris alone and broke off the brief engagement. The two Austen sisters left immediately, though Jane and Cassandra ultimately stayed friends with the Biggs. Harris went on to marry in a few years and have a large family.

Jane still harbored her hopes of having her writing published, and as she traveled she carried all her manuscripts with her for safekeeping. With the help of a lawyer, a friend of her brother Henry, Jane was able to sell *Susan* to Crosby and Son for £10 in 1803. But the publisher, despite promises to publish the novel soon, did nothing. Jane kept writing, working on another novel called *The Watsons*. This novel seemed to involve the theme of marrying for money, with its positives and negatives. It told the story of Emma Watson, who comes from a family with no money and who meets three men—a clergyman, a rich lord, and a popular and handsome young man—at a ball. How Jane intended Emma's life to work out is a mystery since she never completed the story.

Whatever Jane's reason was for leaving *The Watsons* incomplete, her life was soon to be disrupted with major change. Harris had been Jane's last opportunity to marry, and the Austen women, without the financial security that a marriage for Jane or Cassandra would have brought, would soon to find themselves in a difficult situation.

Chapter Five

Sense and Sensibility

"'Sense and Sensibility' I have just finished reading; it certainly is interesting, and you feel quite one of the company."

—Princess Charlotte

In 1804, Jane lost the friend who had first encouraged her in writing, Anne Lefroy. Even if Anne had been at least partly responsible for destroying Jane's hopes of marrying Tom Lefroy years before, the two remained good friends. On Jane's birthday, Anne was riding to a nearby town to do some shopping. On the way home, a riding accident led to her death. From this time on, Jane would associate her birthday with Anne, remembering her friend's life and death.

As the winter went on, another death occurred. Jane's father became ill. A doctor tried to treat him by using hot glass cups pressed against his skin, a technique called "cupping" that aimed to pull blood toward the skin's surface. The treatment was entirely ineffective, and Reverend Austen's health grew worse. On January 21, 1805, he died, passing away quietly in his sleep. His death left his wife and two daughters in extreme financial difficulty. Their only support would come from Jane's brothers, who, between them, offered the women only £400 a year. One quarter of this, £100, came from Frank, but Mrs. Austen only accepted half of the amount from him as he would soon be married and she felt he had offered more than he could afford. The same could not be said for the other sons' offers of support.

Living on only £350 a year was difficult for Mrs. Austen, Cassandra, and Jane. They moved between lodgings, looking for smaller and cheaper ones, but there was no place in Bath that was really within their means. In 1806, one year after Reverend Austen's death, the now-married Frank suggested that his mother and sisters come live with him and his wife in Southampton. As he was in the navy, he was often gone, and Jane, Cassandra, and Mrs. Austen could keep his wife Mary from having to be alone during these long periods of absence. Not only did the three Austen women move in with Frank and Mary, but so did Martha Lloyd, whose mother had just died. Jane would never again return to Bath, happy to be done with the place.

The presence of the three Austen women and Martha was particularly helpful for Frank and Mary in 1807, when Frank was gone at sea and Mary gave birth to her first child. They were also in closer proximity to other relatives now and especially were able to see James and his family more often. Additionally, Edward and his family had begun sometimes staying at an estate he had inherited nearby, Chawton House. Jane enjoyed this nearness to some of her family members, but some, particularly James, she found irritating.

Long visits to friends offered a break from life in Southampton, but without money, Jane could not travel unless one of her brothers or another male relative was going the same way. This sometimes led to difficulties. For example, once she intended to stay at Edward's estate Godmersham for only two weeks, but a change in her escort's plans looked like it would leave her stranded there, over a hundred miles from Southampton, for two months—she would miss the chance to see her friend Catherine Bigg before she married. Jane appealed to Edward, who refused to help her until she resorted to lying about why she needed to go home; even then, he escorted her home with grumbling reminders about how she was wasting his time.

In 1808, for the same reasons, Jane was not able to return to Godmersham when Elizabeth died in childbirth. After Elizabeth's death, two of her and Edward's sons came to stay with Jane and Cassandra for a while—Jane found activities to distract them from their grief, like a rowboat ride and a trip to see a battleship under construction. Her nieces and nephews would later remember Jane as the aunt who told fairy stories and let them play dress-up with her clothes.

When Frank and Mary wanted to have their own home in 1809, they found a house on the Isle of Wight. Once again, the Austen women and Martha Lloyd needed somewhere to live. This time, the wealthy Edward offered them two choices of houses he owned: a house in Kent or a one in Hampshire. Jane, Cassandra, and Martha preferred the Hampshire option, and so the women moved into Chawton Cottage, near Edward's second estate, Chawton House. The cottage was a sizable house by today's standards, with two parlors and six bedrooms.

As the women settled in, Mrs. Austen enjoyed spending her time working in the gardens. Jane found that the cottage felt like home to her, as no place since the move to Bath had. She got up early and played the piano before making breakfast for everyone. She began to write diligently again, as she had not for the last few difficult years. She sent an inquiry—under an assumed name—to the publishers Crosby and Son about the fate of her novel *Susan* and received the discouraging news that they had no intention of publishing it any time soon. She could buy it back for the £10 the publishers had paid, suggested Richard Crosby. This was a sum that Jane could certainly not afford, so she turned to her other writings.

She submitted *Sense and Sensibility* to another publisher, Thomas Egerton. Egerton said he would publish the novel, but Jane would have to pay the printing costs to minimize Egerton's risk. Again, Jane simply could not afford this offer. Fortunately, Henry and Eliza helped Jane out and paid for the novel's printing. Thus Jane began the slow process of seeing one of her novels move toward print for the first time. She was able to examine the proofs for the novel in 1811, while she stayed in London with Henry and Eliza. At last, in the fall of the same year, the novel came out in print. It was originally published anonymously and divided into three volumes.

The book immediately garnered attention, receiving two good reviews that praised the book for its moral lessons, its carefully drawn, lifelike characters, and its believable plot. Women of high society began to read Jane's story of cautious, practical Elinor and her sister, the passionate, enthusiastic Marianne. Even the teenage Princess Charlotte wrote about the novel in a letter to a friend. Within about a year and half, all the copies of the novel that Thomas Egerton had printed had sold. Jane Austen at last had some money of her own—£140. Beyond that, Egerton offered to pay for another book by the same author and gave Jane £110 for *First Impressions*. Jane Austen's future as an author was finally looking up.

Chapter Six

Pride and Prejudice

"I do not want people to be very agreeable, as it saves me the trouble of liking them a great deal."

—Jane Austen

Egerton soon came across a problem with the title *First Impressions*—another book had already been published with the same title. Consequently, Jane had to change the title to *Pride and Prejudice*, perhaps inspired by the ending of Fanny Burney's novel *Cecilia*, a book Austen had liked when she was young, which concluded: "The whole of this unfortunate business has been the result of pride and prejudice." In any case, Jane Austen's *Pride and Prejudice* was released in January 1813.

The story of Elizabeth Bennet and Mr. Darcy's romance immediately found an enthusiastic audience. It was published anonymously, advertised as "By the Author of *Sense and Sensibility*." The novel soon found acclaim with critics and readers alike. One critic wrote that it was "very far superior" to other similar novels of the time. Not everyone loved the book, though—one contemporary of Austen's, writer Mary Russell Mitford, felt that Elizabeth and the scoundrel Mr. Wickham were such a good fit for one another that she was annoyed to see Elizabeth end up with "that delightful Darcy" in the end. Jane herself playfully criticized the book, too, complaining that "the work is rather too light and bright and sparkling" and that it ought to have some long, boring sections unrelated to the plot to weigh it down so that readers could return even more happily to the story.

Jane's family found the finished novel delightful, as they had the original version of *First Impressions*. Even some of the naval officers who knew Jane's youngest brother, Charles Austen, read the book. Though Jane continued trying to keep her name as the author of *Pride and Prejudice* a secret from the public, her identity began to spread. The Austen family did not always help keep the secret—Jane reported that she had heard her brother Henry, in excitedly praising the book, reveal her identity more than once.

The spring after the publication of her second book, Jane traveled to London with Edward's oldest son. There, she arrived at Henry and Eliza's home to nurse Eliza, who was suffering from a fatal disease. Modern scholars believe Eliza may have had breast cancer—the same illness that her mother died from. By the end of April 1813, Eliza died. She would be greatly missed by her family—"a woman of brilliant generous and cultivated mind" was Henry's description of his wife in the epitaph he wrote.

Though Jane left London after Eliza's death, Henry soon asked her to return. In May, Jane and Henry spent time together and visited art exhibitions. Jane amused herself by looking for paintings that could be images of her characters, spotting one that reminded her exactly of the way she pictured Jane Bennet, down to the "white gown, with green ornaments, which convinces me of what I had always supposed, that green was a favourite colour with her." However, she found no painting that seemed like an image of Elizabeth Bennet, and she playfully decided that Mr. Darcy would put too much value on Elizabeth's portraits to let them be shown in an exhibition.

Within her family, Jane was now the older aunt giving advice to her nieces. She advised Fanny, who turned 20 the year that *Pride and Prejudice* was published, not to accept a gentleman who might have been considering proposing to her unless "you really do like him." Jane told her niece that anything would be better than marriage "without affection." To Anna, who was also 20 in 1813, Jane gave advice about writing and developing interesting and consistent characters.

Jane was still writing herself, and her next novel, *Mansfield Park*, would have a more somber tone than her previous works. The early 1800s were troubled times for England politically, as the country was constantly in or on the verge of war with France. As the French expanded their control over other parts of Europe, the British hoped to stop this expansion and maintain the stability of Europe. The British kept Napoleon from invading Russia in 1812, and in 1813 won a battle against Napoleon in Germany. Napoleon was defeated in 1815 in the famous Battle of Waterloo. Britain's attempts to stop the United States from trading with France had also spurred the three-year-long War of 1812.

Meanwhile, Britain's internal politics were also troubled. Many were ashamed of the prince regent, who married his cousin Caroline of Brunswick for money. Both were known for having other lovers, and the prince declared that Caroline was unfit to mother their daughter Charlotte and separated the princess from her mother. The prince's brother, William, the Duke of Clarence, also was involved in scandal. Many British people were shocked by the behavior of their royalty. They believed that the upper classes should be setting an example of good behavior for the rest of society, and especially for the young, yet they saw the opposite happening.

Mansfield Park reflects the grave atmosphere of a country at war and the sober moral concerns of many British people. Out of Jane Austen's completed works, it has almost certainly retained the least popularity today, partly because its plot and characters reflect these issues of Austen's day. Fanny Price is poor and virtuous, while many of the other young characters—her cousins Tom, Maria, and Julia and their friends Henry and Mary Crawford and Mr. Yates—reflect the lack of morals that many saw as a problem among Britain's youth. They are vain, flirt freely, and are more concerned about money than morality.

The decision of the young people to perform a play takes up a significant part of the plot, and Fanny's refusal to take part in it is a major turning point intended to reveal her strength of character. What modern readers might miss is that it is not the act of performing a play that Austen sets up as morally wrong—Jane's brothers enjoyed putting on plays during their young adult years in Steventon—but the play *Lover's Vows* would have been instantly recognizable to Austen's audience as a play improper for youth because it dealt with extramarital sex.

Fanny staunchly hangs on to her moral beliefs in the face of great pressure to marry the wealthy Henry Crawford, ultimately refusing to marry without love. In the end, she is rewarded by marriage to the man she does love, her cousin Edmund. Shy and austere Fanny Price is quite different from the heroine of Austen's previous novel, the quick-witted and playful Elizabeth Bennet. In fact, Mary Crawford, who Jane depicts ultimately as morally lacking, is much more similar to Elizabeth, but unlike Elizabeth, does not develop to be a more thoughtful, self-conscious character. *Mansfield Park* is the work of an older Jane Austen—not the young woman who initially drafted the joyful *First Impressions*, but a woman who had seen her country go through war and had lived through many losses of friends, family (most recently, the death of her brother Charles's wife Frances in 1814), and perhaps even a man whom she hoped to marry.

Mansfield Park was published in 1814, and even at the time, opinions were more mixed than they had been for *Pride and Prejudice*. Her family found some of the characters amusing, but Jane's mother called Fanny Price "insipid," and Cassandra noted that she considered the book "not so brilliant as P. & P." Other readers agreed with Cassandra, though some, like Jane's friend Anne Sharp, praised the strong moral themes of the novel. Nonetheless, the first printing of the book was sold out within half a year. Even with these positive results, Thomas Egerton decided he was not interested in printing more copies of *Mansfield Park*, so even though she had a new novel near completion, it was time for Austen to search for another publisher.

Chapter Seven

Emma, the Unlikeable Heroine

"Pictures of perfection, as you know, make me sick and wicked."

—Jane Austen

With her brother Henry's help, Jane soon sold her next novel, *Emma*, to a publisher named John Murray. Murray, enthusiastic about the new book, also purchased the rights to two of Jane's earlier books, *Sense and Sensibility* and *Mansfield Park*. He intended to print new editions of these books later on. When Henry became seriously ill in 1815, Jane began to work with Murray herself instead of through her brother. She traveled to London late that fall for a meeting with her publisher.

One of Henry's physicians was also a court physician, and so the prince regent—a man whom Jane despised, but who liked her work—discovered she was in London. Jane received an invitation to tour the library of the prince's Carlton House in London. There, she met the royal librarian, Reverend James Stanier Clarke, who suggested that she ought to dedicate her forth-coming novel to the prince regent. This sort of suggestion did not really leave

Jane a lot of choice, despite her feelings about the prince, and so she wrote a brief dedication for *Emma* consisting of less than a dozen words.

Murray quickly told Austen that this would not work, and he wrote a different dedication—a longer one more appropriate for royalty. He also printed a special copy of the book to be presented to the prince regent. Jane met the librarian Clarke again when he wanted to thank her on behalf of the prince. He gave her some suggestions for what she could write about next, which Jane turned down with as much politeness as possible, telling Clarke that she could not write about the life of a clergyman as he suggested because she was "the most unlearned and uninformed female who ever dared to be an authoress." Clarke offered further ideas, which Jane did not take either. But she did, in private and for her own amusement, script an outline for a ridiculous story based on Clarke's suggestions. This satirical "Plan of a Novel, According to Hints from Various Quarters" shows Austen's sense of humor and her enjoyment of poking fun at the absurdities she encountered in life.

As she had done with her previous book, Austen wrote down what her friends and family had to say about her new novel *Emma*, first published in December of 1815. Cassandra was pleased, but Jane's mother held onto *Pride and Prejudice* as the best of Jane's works. Fanny Knight, Jane's niece—to whom Jane had read *Pride and Prejudice* aloud—liked Mr. Knightly, but said she "could not bear *Emma* herself." This should not have come as too much of a surprise to Austen, who had famously decided that in writing *Emma*, she would "take on a heroine whom no one but myself will much like."

Jane's statement about her main character may not be completely true—after all, Emma may be at times snobbish, impulsive, and presumptuous, but she is also witty, intelligent, and caring. As in Austen's other novels, the cast of interesting and believable characters and the structure of society drive the narrative, as Emma attempts to play matchmaker for her friend Harriet, encounters misunderstandings and makes serious mistakes, and finally is forced to realize her own love for her friend Mr. Knightly only when she begins to think she has lost him. Many scholars consider *Emma* to be Jane Austen's masterpiece—though, like Jane's family, most readers come to their own opinions. Though Jane did not know it, *Emma* would be the last novel she would publish within her lifetime.

Following *Emma*, John Murray printed another edition of *Mansfield Park*, which came out in February of 1816. As Jane began to make money from her work, she was able to send £10 to buy back the rights to *Susan* from Crosby and Son. Jane decided to change the name "Susan" to "Catherine" throughout the book. But it was clear that she had developed much farther as a writer since 1803 when she had penned *Susan*. No longer feeling that this work was worth publishing, Jane put it, as she told Fanny Knight, "upon the shelve." Without delay, she began work on a new novel, called *The Elliots*.

Chapter Eight

Jane's Mysterious Illness

"Composition seems to me impossible, with a head full of joints of mutton and doses of rhubarb."

—Jane Austen

As Austen kept on writing, many members of her family were going through difficult times. The peace with France, while beneficial for the country as a whole, had negative consequences for those who relied on military and naval careers to earn a living. Jane's brother Charles was particularly impacted. He had been stationed near Naples, and when the war ended, he began working on suppressing Mediterranean piracy. He captured two pirate ships, but then his own ship, a frigate named the HMS *Phoenix*, was shipwrecked near Smyrna (modern-day Izmir, Turkey) in early 1816. Without a war going on, the navy had little motivation to give him command of another ship quickly—in fact, he would have to wait ten years.

In the meantime, he had to support and raise three daughters without the help of a wife; like several of the Austen brothers' wives, Charles' wife Frances had died in childbirth. His struggle with poverty was worsened by the medical care needed to help his middle daughter, Harriet, with her terrible headaches; the doctors treated her with mercury. Jane assumed that young Harriet would die before long, but in fact, Harriet lived several decades longer.

Frank had also made his career in the navy, but he had tried to make investments to help stabilize his income when the war ended. Unfortunately, a part of his investments was in his brother Henry's bank, and the bank collapsed in 1816 due to some risky investments Henry had made during this time when the economic climate was not stable. Frank was not the only member of the family with money at stake; Jane had invested £13 of her earnings from *Mansfield Park* in the bank as well. Henry only weathered the bank's collapse with financial help from Edward and from their mother's wealthy relatives, the Leigh-Perrots. His charisma and likability kept most of the family from being angry with him for too long, with the exception of the Leigh-Perrots. Soon, he decided to start a new career as a clergyman, and before 1816 was over, he became the curate at Chawton.

Though Jane saw her brothers' difficulties as more serious than her own and so did not want to complain, in 1816, she began to experience health problems—mostly aches and pains that she could not attribute to an obvious source. Concerned, Cassandra convinced Jane to go with her to Cheltenham, a spa town, in late spring. There, as in Bath, the mineral waters were reputed to have restorative effects. While there, Jane drank a pint of the mineral water every morning before eating breakfast.

Despite her illness, Austen kept on writing. After returning home, she was often busy with Frank's children and sometimes Charles' oldest daughter, but nonetheless she finished *The Elliots* in July. She was not quite satisfied with the book, however, and soon decided to rewrite the two final chapters.

Jane turned 41 years old in December of 1816 and, as the new year began, declared her health to be improving. She wrote to one of her nieces, explaining that she had been feeling poorly for several weeks, with fevers at times, but was "considerably better now and recovering my looks a little, which have been bad enough, black and white and every wrong colour." She also said that all that was wrong was rheumatism, "just a little pain in my knee now and then." She did not want to give in to illness, which she called "a dangerous indulgence at my time of life," nor did she want others to consider her an invalid and give her special treatment. She refused to lie on the sofa if she felt tired after dinner, not wanting to stop her mother from napping there. Instead, Jane lay across three parlor chairs, which her niece Caroline could not help but notice looked fairly uncomfortable.

After finishing her revisions to *The Elliots*, Jane started on another novel which she called *The Brothers*. This new novel was set in a seaside resort called Sanditon. But in spite of Austen's efforts to carry on with life as usual and fight against her suffering health, by March of 1817, she felt too ill to continue writing and stopped work on the manuscript, which was then 12 chapters long. Jane still urged Cassandra to go to be with their Aunt Leigh-

Perrot when her husband, their uncle, died at the end of March. The Austens must have hoped for an inheritance from their wealthy uncle, but he left them little—and nothing at all for Mrs. Austen, his sister, who had little enough to live on already. Jane's health soon worsened, and she asked Cassandra to come home again.

Chapter Nine

Last Days and Death

"Mr. Lyford says he will cure me, and if he fails, I shall draw up a memorial and lay it before the Dean and Chapter, and have no doubt of redress from that pious, learned, and disinterested body."

—Jane Austen

No-one knows exactly what disease Jane Austen suffered from at the end of her life. Some have speculated that it might have been Addison's disease, which causes the body's adrenal glands to produce insufficient amounts of hormones. Today, this disease is treated by having patients take hormones to replace those the body is not producing, but in Austen's day, the disease would have been a mystery. Symptoms vary but include fatigue, discolored skin, and muscle or joint pain—symptoms that seem to match some of the recorded details of Jane's illness. However, it is hard to come to any secure conclusion. It is possible that Jane had one of a number of other illnesses; some have rejected the idea of Addison's disease and instead suggested that she could have had Hodgkin's lymphoma or tuberculosis.

In any case, when her nieces Caroline and Anna called at Chawton Cottage soon after Cassandra's return, they were taken aback by Jane's appearance—pale, suffering, with a weak voice, and generally looking incapacitated. Jane's illness grew worse as April went on, and her concerned family at last brought a surgeon, Mr. Lyford, to see her. Aloud, Austen said that his treatments were benefiting her. Privately, she recorded her will on April 27; she left everything that she had or might later receive—minus expenses for a funeral and £50 each for Henry and Madame Bigeon, one of Henry's servants who had long served the family and been financially injured by Henry's bank collapsing—to her "dearest sister Cassandra Elizabeth."

Eventually, Jane gave in and agreed that she should go to Winchester to be under Mr. Lyford's care. She and Cassandra set out near the end of May, traveling in James and Mary's carriage. Jane still had the energy to comment on the fact that she did not see Mary as "a liberal-minded woman" despite the loan of the carriage—she had never come to love having Mary as her sister-in-law. Henry and one of Jane's nephews traveled along as well, riding on horseback by the carriage even though it was raining. Jane was grateful for her family's concern.

The two sisters rented a room together on College Street. Jane continued to insist that she would get better, but at the beginning of June, Cassandra asked Mary to come help. Mary's diary records her observations of Jane's health—which drastically declined in just half a week. The family did not expect Jane to recover at this point. However, Jane did, seeming to improve significantly, so much so that Mary left and went home. But this seemingly miraculous recovery did not last; just days later, Jane and Cassandra needed Mary once again.

July 15 was St. Swithin's Day, on which the town of Winchester planned to hold a series of races. Unfortunately, the day was rainy. Jane, ever imaginative, dictated a poem to Cassandra in which St. Swithin curses the people for holding races for fun on his holy day, causing the rain. After this, Jane's energy and strength went downhill quickly. Two days later, on July 17, 1817, her pain was so intense that Lyford gave her a potent drug to help. Early in the morning of the 18th, Jane Austen died in Cassandra's arms. Cassie mourned the loss of her sister deeply, comparing Jane's death to losing a part of herself.

Almost a week after her death, Austen's body was buried in Winchester Cathedral. Several of her brothers and one of her nephews traveled to attend. James, who was ill and could not travel, wrote a poem in tribute of his sister, praising her mind and quick wit. Jane's brother, who wrote the inscription for her tombstone, also praised her mind and her sweetness. Whether her temper really was quite as amiable as her family's remembrances make it out to have been is impossible to know. Her writings certainly reveal a woman who was willing to make witty observations and sometimes cutting remarks about her society and human nature, and it is difficult to imagine that, as James' poem claimed, her wit "never gave offense."

Many of Austen's letters, of which she wrote over 3,000, were lost. Some were destroyed, like Cassandra's.

Others were lost in other ways; for example, when Frank died almost 50 years after Jane, his daughter threw away his collection of Jane's letters. While the family did not realize what an important writer Jane had been, they did see value in Jane's unpublished works.

At the end of 1817, Austen's two finished but unpublished works were published together. *Catherine*, the book that Jane had shelved when she finally bought it back from the publisher, was published as *Northanger Abbey*. The other was *The Elliots*, Jane's last novel, which was called *Persuasion* when it was printed. *Persuasion* is the story of the oldest of Jane's heroines, Anne Elliot, who was persuaded not to marry the man she loved when she was young. Years later she still loves him, and in the course of the novel, she is offered a second chance: "She had been forced into prudence in her youth, she learned romance as she grew older—the natural sequence of an unnatural beginning."

The novel Austen had begun during her illness, *The Brothers*, was left unfinished upon her death. It was published in its incomplete form as *Sanditon* in 1925 and has left Jane Austen's fans speculating about what would have happened ever since.

Conclusion

Not only were Austen's remaining two novels published posthumously, but her work was soon translated into French. However, it would still be many years before Jane Austen became a household name; the readership for her works was fairly small for several decades after her death. In 1869, this quickly changed. One of Jane's nephews, James Edward Austen-Leigh, wrote the first biography of Jane, called *A Memoir of Jane Austen*, using family memories and surviving letters. This biography pushed Jane Austen's name into the limelight, and her popularity has continued to grow ever since.

Jane Austen's works have not only proved to be memorable in and of themselves but have consistently inspired other writers—from Rudyard Kipling's "The Janeites," a story about soldiers in World War I who read Jane Austen's novels for encouragement, to the 2009 comedy film *Pride and Prejudice and Zombies*. Several authors have attempted to provide a satisfying finish to the tale of Charlotte Heywood that Jane began in *Sanditon*; most famous of these is Marie Dobb's 1975 version (published in different editions under the pseudonyms "Another Lady" and "Anne Telscombe"). Many imaginative sequels to Austen's novels have appeared, and her work has even inspired films such as *Clueless* (1995), based on *Emma*. Jane Austen Societies encourage the study of Austen's work in the U.K., Australia, and North America, and the U.K. society has worked to preserve Jane's home at Chawton Cottage as well as other artifacts related to the Austens.

Jane Austen's enduring legacy is seen in the way she wrote about everyday people with playful humor and penetrating insight. As biographer Helen Lefroy writes, even though the structure of modern society is quite different than the times that Austen wrote in, "everyone recognises the situations she deals with. She showed that a writer doesn't have to go to big, topical or historical themes in order to be relevant: there's plenty of human material right in front of you."

Made in the USA
Lexington, KY
06 January 2019